I0503241

Turning 30 Seconds Into 1 Hour
Time Management

Copyright 2018 By John Boom
ISBN: 978-1-387-89358-4

About

They say time is relative to how you use it. So if we could actually turn say 30 seconds of thought into 1 hour of value time savings wouldn't that change your life? Time management can change your business and your personal life if managed differently for many people.

So I wrote this book to help those look at different perspectives in their lives. For those that are at home, school and for those that work or own a business time management can be a major factor in your life. How you manage your time can relate directly to the quality of your lifestyle.

Index

Turning 30 Seconds Into 1 Hour
Time Management

They say time is relative to how you use it. So if we could actually turn say 30 seconds of thought into 1 hour of value time savings wouldn't that change your life? Time management can change your business and your personal life if managed differently for many people.

In business and in fact in many things we do in life how we manage our time means the difference between getting more or less done. So I thought I'd write a little about how I manage my time. And it may just work for you too.

Currently I run around 35 websites and groups, I'm a singer and songwriter, I've written several books and many papers, I run a 6 day per week factory and sales warehouse, I have a family, I've produced AustralianPictorials.com filming nearly every Australian town, I manufacture my own products to my own clothing label like ladies bags, jewellery, disks, books, my art works on to canvas and I've produced over 2,000 videos on my Youtube Chanel.

And in doing all these things I find I have plenty of time to still do plenty of other things. You may think

I'm a busy person but to me time goes much slower because of the way I manage my time and how I process my concepts.

In the past during my life I worked in all manner of jobs so I have collected a vast experience in many areas which to me has always been like an adventure. And like many others I've had to work in jobs I hated or do things I didn't want to do because I had a family to support. These days my kids have left the nest and have lives of their own but we've still ended up taking full time care of our young disabled granddaughter. So life has its challenges and for us it's been no exception.

I've always worked hard and as a family we've always had to battle through the good and bad times many of which very difficult times in our lives. Life is a struggle for most people unless you had a rich benefactor and even then wealthy people don't always have such good lives either. Life has many challenges along its journey. Sickness or bad health can affect anyone and I'm no exception as these days I have a pacemaker in place which keeps me ticking over. So I feel as I'm nothing special and anything I achieved I had to work very hard for.

Hitting hard times when we were younger and become like homeless gypsies with kids in tow we had to live in sheds and caravans until we finally managed to build our own home from bits and pieces finally finding a job to even working at trash and treasure markets to help make a few extra bucks toward buying building materials as we could afford them.

It breaks my heart these days seeing so many homeless people and not being able to say to them there is a future for you but you have to make it happen for yourselves as we had to do. I've written many articles on how to help those less fortunate as well but it's not easy breaking through the barrier of corrupt governments these days as I'm sure many of you may know.

After having many years of a difficult life and personal family issues we persevered and I gradually developed my way in life of doing things differently. A hard life can in fact force you to develop different skills you may have thought you never had.

It's not something everyone can do and I fully understood that. And as some years progressed my life started changing because I developed a different way of thinking which enabled me to do things very differently. So now being in my sixties I thought I'd try and expand some of my concepts to perhaps help some others find their way too. This is not about making you a millionaire it's about changing concepts and the way you think about getting the most back from your time.

And I suppose if you have some luck and extra motivation it may well help you do much better in life. I've written other books on helping people do better in business and this book isn't solely about that. This book is about time management concepts. It's about showing you different ways of thinking so you can achieve much more in your available time. And time is always slipping away from all of us as we get older. So having some sort of system in place to be able to make better use of that time may help some people more than others.

It's all about your state of mind and how you can train your mind to do tasks. Every time you sleep in and put off jobs you know those jobs will still be there for you to do no matter how hard you try and get out of it. We all do this and I'm no exception. We all choose how much time we want to allocate to the jobs we do.

I've found that early in the morning while still in bed I start planning my day. I organize sections of time into productive periods of work time in my thoughts. If I want to write a song for instance before I start writing it I already put the concept of the tune into my mind. It could say be just the title.

Then when I get into my work place I can just extend my song concept from the title of the song. Rather than spend a whole week writing song I can write the song usually in about 5 minutes and then I just adjust pieces of the song to how I want it. After that I add the music to suit the tune. The whole process may only take up to a half an hour from the first concept to the finished song.

That's a huge time saving for every song when you work things out that way. So when you apply the same concept of time management with concept thought you can do the same with most tasks you want to do. For instance if you're building an addition onto your home you can plan what you need to do by planning it all down to having all your tools and materials organized in your mind before you even start your job.

Rather than just go to the work site and fumble around for hours going from one place to another, thinking about it as you go. After having all those items in your mind all you need to do when you're at the building site is collect the items you thought about. The mind works fast and sometimes it only takes seconds to remind yourself what you need to do in specific tasks. If you have to write down notes to help remind you.

So those seconds of thought can turn into time savings on the building site. Your thought will give you the chance to know what you'll need to do and where to go to get those items. That's got to save to you time right?

Time Management Thought Planning

If you organize the way you think your organized thought can sometimes take hours out of many jobs. It all sounds so simple when you think about it. **Time management thought planning** can save you hours of time in a week leaving you spare time to manage other jobs and have spare time for recreation.

I can go from one task to another and have it done in a shorter space of time than most simply because every job and task has been organized in my minds filing cabinet. Seeing what you're looking at is very important as well because you need to know your task requirements. If you don't know what you're doing you'll be stuffing around for ages. So it pays to do any research you need to know well in advance or do what I do and that is nut it out in your subconscious so you can see how to do each task in your mind's eye first. Just think about it.

Then when you physically start the job you've already nutted out the best way to do each task. This way you've already taught yourself how to do a job because you've used your mind to teach you the most logical way to perform each task. You'll find once you start with this line of thinking you're actually teaching yourself how to work every time before you even start any job. They say life is a learning curve and this is exactly what you're doing. Everyday you'll teach yourself how to be more time efficient with every task you do.

If you have websites for instance like myself I have to manage many multiple groups and websites and I already know in my mind this is the way I'll go about servicing all those sites. It reduces the management time if you work your mind in that way of thinking. Sometimes you may need to say add photos, take photos and reduce the quality and size of them. Add information for other people. Check through a host of emails from different email addresses from different websites. And the list can be very large sometimes in regards to what needs to be done.

The before-time mind-planning will categorize all those jobs into time effective work periods instead of just sitting there and then thinking about what to do every day which can add many hours to every job. Productive up front thinking and planning may give you hours to spare during your day to extra days in your week. So say using 30 seconds of thought planning may give you an hour or more of time savings for many tasks.

Advanced thought planning can save you a lot of time if you can teach yourself how to apply that thought into practice. Every time you try and short cut the planning process you'll most likely find it will take you longer to do every task. Because you never planned it out in your mind in advance and you'll find your decision making process is delayed into making spot decisions every time.

Then you'll find yourself jumping from one place to another with unplanned jobs mounting up as you go. Naturally when you're thinking behind the ball as it were each time simple tasks can end up taking you hours longer to perform.

You'll find yourself distracted by say having to go in the middle of a job to say buy some more materials or supplies. You may have been able to do those jobs beforehand at a better time. Every time you go away from your job you may again get distracted and before you know it half the morning or afternoon is gone.

So that advanced thinking and planning which sometimes may only take seconds of thought can actually save your hours of your day. When you work for an employer or if you are an employer the same concepts can be applied if that's within your control to do so. I've found that if you're an employer for instance having your daily tasks set out in your mind you try and plan them in such a way that again you have everything in place for people to do in a time cost effective way so it can save you money by getting more done within each day from each employee.

For instance if you can reel back an extra two hours of production work each day just by planning in advance in how you organize production that's a huge saving over a year. That may mean more income produced from having the same people and more time to produce more finished product or services and so forth. Simply recognizing you say need to have components organized by say one person so others don't have to waste time thinking about that are areas where you can save heaps of time over a large workforce. Massive time savings can be had this way.

Things don't organize themselves so you need to organize them. If you already know what your production requirements are upfront you can have all that in place ready to go rather let your staff waste "your paid time" on doing that. If you're a manufacturer there are huge savings to be made in these areas. Again 30 seconds or so of thought can save you lots of wasted time by others. Many of us wake up say an hour earlier in the mornings but you still stay in bed so why waste that time thinking about nothing.

Put your mind into planning mode each morning so you can save hours or whatever time is possible from each day in advance. If you're in the retail industry you should know certain jobs always need doing like stock replacement, cleaning, organizing, and opening new deliveries and much more. Use those early morning wake times and see yourself in all the jobs that need to be done each day beforehand.

Then when you get into the work place you can delegate or organize jobs for people to do to save time in other areas of work practice. Otherwise you'll be depending on them to do that and by the time they think of many things you've lost valuable time which you could have used in many other areas.

Using these methods isn't all about trying to work at excessive speeds it's about taking up the slack in time it takes to think about doing things. Basically wasted time most people would never even think about.

I'll give you an example. If you have people that say sew clothing for you then you can have an advanced pile of ready cut pattern pieces next to their machine ready to use first thing when they sit down at the machine. They don't have to get up and bother you or find out where those stock items may be because it's all there thought out for them. Having people or yourself wasting time always looking after the fact means you're losing time in your day that you could have used to do many other things.

People waste a huge part of their day aimlessly thinking about things as they do them rather than thinking about those things before they do them. Advanced planning and thinking can save you a lot a valuable time. For those of us that are what we call time poor this can make a huge difference in your life.

If you find yourself stressing because you have little time to set aside to do other more enjoyable things in life I put it to you to try my methods of pre-thinking your day before it actually starts. Thinking your day through shouldn't be an exhausting process. It's about streamlining your operations into thought patterns that you can place into little blocks of information that you set time saving tasks for yourself and others to do before you actually do them.

Planning your day is just like you would say plan an event like say a wedding. You don't leave things to chance and you organize everything in such a way it becomes like a routine. Everything must be accounted for so you have an organized method of placing things in place so the day runs as smoothly as possible. Naturally things can always go wrong as unexpected things happen.

But if you plan all your work projects well even if something goes wrong chances are you many still have time on your side because good planning saves time in many other areas too. No system is infallible. Because you can re-organize the way you do things and still save lots of hours over a day, week and year you'll always still be upfront. You always have to take the good with the bad.

You should also look at how you operate in the first instance because many people don't always have good mental and physical skills. This is why people do courses, go to schools, do apprenticeships, copy others or whatever. There's nothing wrong with teaching yourself to be better at what you want to do. You can never learn too much.

You may find doing a course related to the field of work you're in may help you cope better with those jobs. I've been so lucky in my life as I've been able to develop concepts and teach myself new skills but not everyone can do that and you should never feel uncomfortable to ask for help. Most people will go out of their way to help you. Why I'm saying all of this is that to be able to save the time you need to know all the facets of your job. It's harder to plan for something you don't know how to do because like baking a cake you won't know the ingredients.

Especially if you're an employer because you need to make it your job to know and understand many of the jobs that need doing in the workplace otherwise you'll have no hope of planning ahead for your employees. Like for instance if you worked in a factory and you had to set aside pieces of material components for say a stamping machine you'd have to know exactly which parts to have ready for that operator to use. You have to make it your job to know all the functions of the industry you work in.

Plus many employees work to timetables in production so if you make up those timetables you'd know they'd need specific materials and time to carry out those tasks every day.

Having those materials at hand when they need them saves time. That time you save can mean more production or more time to do other tasks you may want to do be they personal or work related. You pay employees by the hour so I'm sure you'd know for every hour in time they have to waste waiting for things means you still have to pay them for that wasted time.

I hate paying for wasted time so I make sure everything my employees need is ready and waiting for them on each different job even if I have to delegate others to get that done. No one is saying you're superman so delegate jobs out as you need too. Make the best of your skills to out think others before they need back-up materials. Paying for down time can be wasteful.

Getting A Good Night's Sleep

Getting a good night sleep is so important because if you don't sleep well you'll have trouble functioning the next morning. You may be prone to sleeping in for instance. Well that leaves you no time to think in advance on how to plan for your day. That day as far as time savings goes may be down the toilet. Having that early morning thinking advantage is where you profit from your upcoming day.

In time you'll find early morning pre-thinking won't be so crucial depending on what type of work you do. If your work is basically a similar routine and nothing much changes you'll be skimming much of the pre-thinking process because you'll know exactly what to do each day before each day starts.

But many jobs like say on a building site may be totally different every day and it may involve a whole host of variables. Naturally those variables can and will affect you so you need to learn how to read the future of those events. With experience you'll learn to work around those variables as they occur and that too will become second nature to you because you'll become a good problem solver.

Because people that think in advance teach themselves how to adapt better than people that just plod along. Because they're forced to only think at the time of what they do. You'll always be

thinking a step ahead of them. In many cases you may be thinking a week in front of them always knowing what needs to be done before it happens. You can make it happen how you plan it once you get into a regular habit of thinking in advance and pre-empting the things that need to be done. People in the work place may think you can read minds if you become good at time management. Your mind will be in sync with what needs to be done. I was always out thinking my bosses in the workplace. You can teach yourself to do the same.
I even redesigned machinery and manufacturing processes.

Time Management

It all seems so practical and easy to do but unless you keep thinking in advance you'll find yourself falling back into wasteful time loss. The world revolves around routine. The buses and trains come at certain times, planes leave at certain times and many things you do during the day starts at certain times.

You may say these are all fixed time things that you can't change. That may be true for things out of your control but things that are in your control you can change. So you need to start thinking in more flexible terms when it comes to time management. You can change this within your control to suit specific conditions.

In the work place for instance your workers may be used to a specific start time, morning break time, lunch time, afternoon break time and finish time. If you're the boss you may say I can't rock the boat and we must stick to those specific times because they're set in stone. But that may not always be the case. If you employ a lot of people for instance it may pay you to split work programs into different times so you can continue production during each day.

For example let a percentage of workers go on their morning break first and then let the other percentage of workers go on their break when the first team of workers come back. That way you continue production saving time and increasing production over a whole day. Over a year that can make a huge difference. If everyone stops nothing is being produced but if you stagger the all the breaks during a day you still keeping the wheel turning and at the same time you're satisfying the needs of your workers. It can also let some catch up.

It doesn't place any more pressure on workers at all. Again your job is to pre-empt the needs of the second stage of workers so they have all the ready supply of components they may need during those different break times. I hope you can see how different this approach can make to your business and workplace. If you're in business you still have to pay your workers no matter what but to have your whole work team idle and stopped at break times is just poor economics. So don't be scared to break your workforce into different operating teams. If some workers are sick and away from work you must already have a balanced contingency program waiting in the wings for in those break times so you balance the work output to be in line with production output.

If you don't do that you may find some sectors of the workplace may be waiting on materials for the others to produce. That means wasted down time. So you have to pre-empt those very normal occurrences that most businesses must face on a regular basis. So here you are changing what you thought couldn't be changed. Your life and your business isn't a bus leaving the same time every day from a bus stop. It can be managed, manipulated, altered, and controlled to your advantage.

The House Person

The need of everyone is different and again time management for some people would change their whole life. People may have set routines every week for doing the washing, cleaning, preparing meals, getting the kids off to school, shopping, paying bills and list may be very long for many. So let's see how we can change some of that to give you more time.

As I stated planning your jobs before you get out of bed in your early morning wake time you spend in bed is a good time to think about how you do things during the day. I did that this morning before I came to work and started writing some more in this book. I already decided I was going to put a couple of specific topics in the book. It took me less than 20 seconds to decide that. That will save me an hour or more of planning if I were just to rock up at work with no clue what to do. I don't want to be spending time researching if I can spend a few seconds doing that in bed with some thought time. I hate wasting time.

Again as I said earlier your daily routines may not be fixed in stone so you can adjust and manipulate your own outcomes to give yourself more time to do other things. You may be currently be weighted down in your life thinking everything I do is such a chore and I have no spare time for anything or anyone. It may have got to the stage when it's depressing you into a fixed line of thinking that life can't get any better for you. If this is you let's see if we can change some of that to your advantage.

Writing Down Your Routine

In a domestic situation you may be able to document your daily routines you currently have in place for the whole week. This is a good starting point. You then need to highlight the things you do that may be fixed tasks that you can't vary due to specific outside requirements like say having the kids at school at specific times. So do that first and let's see how we can make some changes.

Okay remember the part in the book where I spoke about employees and changing their break times to give you a better production output system. Well now I'll adapt that for you in a household situation. Let's first tackle some of those things you think are set in stone and that you think you can't change. I put it to you they may be changed under the right conditions and I'll show you what I mean with some examples.

So you may say dropping kids of at school is a fixed time thing right? So let's look at that differently. For some people they could lose an hour of more just getting through traffic to get the kids on their way each morning and the same at night. So let's look at some different planning options.

What if you got together with some other parents in your area and car pooled some kids together? Even if that is for a couple of days a week that would be saving you some hours of travel every week giving you some extra free time. You could set up a parents or carer club from people near your area going to the same school and again do the same thing allocating travel between many of yourselves. The more you can organize the more freed up time you may have. You don't have to isolate yourself in life.

Again if your kids take the bus you may be able to arrange some other parents to take it in turn taking and watching kids at the bus stop. Again it can free up more time for you again.

You make up a time table between the people you can organize and use that as best you can to manipulate the jobs you thought were fixed in time. The same process can be applied perhaps to some other tasks like say if you need just a few things at the shop perhaps the same group could take on those tasks and in return you offer the same for them. Over a week this alone could free up many hours of running around and travel times.

Well we all have to eat and make meals so you know you may have fixed times for that too right? Preparing meals like everything takes time so you may also know that to prepare say several meals for extra people really doesn't add that much extra work or time as the basics are usually always the same. So let's take all of that some steps further.

If you prepare say a mixed rice dinner for one night then why not make enough for the whole family for two, three of more nights and then freeze it in meal night sized family bags? If you did this with many varied meals you could in fact prepare a whole range of variety meals in advance freeing up all those preparation meal times you would normally do daily. You can stagger how often you do this depending on when you need extra time the most.

The contents of some lunches could be prepared that way as well. Like say cooked chicken for chicken sandwiches. You could boil a few eggs for lunches or dinner in advance. The options are endless once you get the idea of preparing some bulk meals instead of just one at a time every day. All these techniques can give you more time during each day to do other things.

So taking the kids to school and preparing meals all may have seem fixed time jobs which you couldn't change but as you can see by my examples it may just be possible to change those after all.

The easier things to change are cleaning and washing times. And how you can manipulate all of those jobs can vary massively. It really is endless how you can swap things around to make them more time saving around the home.

Delegating jobs to others is another way to free up more time for you. Sometimes people may consider paying someone to say do jobs like say mowing the lawns, ironing, cleaning, doing the washing, weeding the garden etc.

So how much is having some extra free time worth to you in dollar terms? That you need to decide for yourself I can't advise you on that. Sometimes paying someone to do some tasks can mean valuable time for you to do other things. The cost may be well worth that to you especially if you find yourself time poor.

Sometimes you can swap time with others and do a little time bartering to gain some time for things you really want to do. It's not a cop out to approach others to do this because you'll probably find they're in the same position as you. Even setting up a time management club on say Facebook could pay off big time in your area for all concerned and you may make some extra friends along the way. Not everything is cut and dry and you should always leave your options open for change.

Again before you get up each morning while still lying awake in bed rather than waste that time thinking about very little use that time more productively and think about how you're going to manage your tasks. If you think you need specific materials to do your job make sure you have them beforehand. Don't forget Internet shopping online can save you heaps of time as well. I buy thousands of items over a year in my business.

Habits And Routines

It's so easy to just take what you do each day for granted because it's what you've been doing for years perhaps. And many of us know breaking bad habits become like addictions and they can be very hard to change. You may drive to work the same way everyday even though going a different way may be faster for instance. And everything you do each day may have a better more time effective way of doing the same thing each day thereby it could save you lots of valuable time you could be using for other things.

Sometimes it needs to be pointed out to you that preparing for each day in advance is like planning for a holiday in that you need to make sure you have everything with you that you need to make that journey. Working and doing tasks at home each day is no different all. It's all about advanced preparation and using better organizational skills.

You know for instance if you have to peel potatoes you'll need to have potatoes in stock to do that. No good waiting to start any job and then find you don't have any of what you need. The same applies to say mowing the grass as you already know you may need fuel.

So before you start any job during the day plan what you need to have beforehand so that can save you a lot of time and running around. Better to go say early in the morning to a hardware store when it's not so busy than wait and find out you need to go during the day because you didn't plan your day of supplies needed upfront. Planning your daily needs earlier beforehand can save you lots of time during the day. Spending 30 seconds of thinking time early in the morning for instance can save you a lot of wasted time during the day.

Every Day Is Not The Same

Every day at work or in the home isn't always the same so some days may need a little more planning than others. If you know up front you need to check materials before you start any task it's better to do that that really early in the day because you don't want to say run out of paint in the middle of painting. That would be a huge inconvenience right? So be prepared to think your day out as required to suit every job that needs to be done during each day.

Time management and task management is about planning for the unforeseen events that can make your day intolerable. It adds stress in your life and who needs more stress these days. Things are hard enough in life so go out of your way to break your old routine of just plodding along each day without any planning at all. Start planning from now on.

Imagine you're preparing for a race and you need to psych yourself up each day before you get out of bed. Because a small amount of thinking can help you plan your day out much better if you've imagined all the things you need to have and do for the upcoming day.   Preparation is everything to save time during each day. It doesn't have to be a race and it's not always about making a profit as its about making a difference in your life to give you time to step back and do other things you're interested in doing.

Having more time to spend with your family for instance or getting work done sooner so you can say just have a walk. It's about improving the quality of your personal life and perhaps for others around you. In business it can regulate or streamline work practices. It can increase profitability. It can give you more production or other time to do different or extra things. No matter what you use your extra saved time for it's for your benefit and perhaps that of others. We all need quality time and sometimes the burden of everything around us clouds that perception and we may forget about preparation and time management.

Multi-tasking

Multitasking tasks is required these days both on the job and in the home. The more you can do the more useful you can be. It doesn't mean you'll be more productive it just means you can do more different things. Let's face it you can only do one job at a time but being able to do many things makes you more useful.

In employment for instance you may be able to work several different machines which means at break times you can take over for another operator. If a person is sick you can take over their job to take their place till they come back.

If you have your own business you must learn to prioritize, set goals and delegate work to others to save yourself lots of time. You can't always do everything yourself. You must teach yourself how to leverage other people's time to your advantage. So delegating jobs to others under time guidelines couldn't be more important otherwise you'll be operating at a loss in no time.

You must develop cost effective ways into whatever you produce to make the finished product cost effective. That's where your profit margin is in the finished product. If you waste too much time making a product there'll be no profit margin left in your products and you'll be operating at a loss.

In business you're investing your time and money into every task that takes place. Using trial and error to run your business isn't a good place to be in this is why you always need to make sure you have the relevant experience at hand. If that means training yourself or having others working for you that are trained so be it as that's a part of running a successful business. Trial and error usually only adds up to a loss.

Using machinery can be a huge time saving tool because you can usually turn out more production as machines don't get tired and just keep working as long as you keep them maintained. People also need to be maintained. So you need to strike a balance of what you can afford and how automated your operations become. Going too far in debt just to save some time may not always be the right balance. Sometimes it can cost too much money to save a little time so you have to choose the right balance you can afford.

Using the right leverage can further your business to get more done or in less time or with less effort. Technology and machinery can be your best tool to upgrade your business if it's within your means. Manufacturing output is obviously a huge factor in any business. Making more time available using such technology means more output and profits if you have the market for those sales. So as you can see time is a valuable resource to everyone.

Humans are always running out of time because we place barriers in our own lives that state we must always try and do better. Working smarter in the home and on the business front obviously may save you time and make you more money. Take advantage of others around you to help reach your time saving goals. Usually it's a symbiotic relationship where most parties will benefit. Like say having good experienced working staff as they will get paid well and you get the benefits of their best work.

Planning your goals and daily work practices is about reward. You must focus your attention on doing what will give you the best and most reliable returns each time. You can't always do everything yourself and even in business many of us outsource parts of jobs to others. This may mean you don't have to buy say specialized equipment or have specially trained staff in other areas.

For instance in our business I outsource our canvas art printing because I don't have room for such a large machine and I may only require a limited stock amount at any time. So it's more cost and time effective to outsource those jobs to others. So leveraging their time, skills and machinery works out much more cost and time effective for me and everyone wins that way.

Training Yourself And Your Staff

It's always an investment in yourself and business if you're well informed and trained in anything you want to undertake. In business the same applies to your staff. Spending the time training staff usually means a higher level of productivity so it's a good investment to do this.

Naturally you can't always personally learn every trade and do every job so having experienced people working around you can only strengthen your business. In the home front it's the same as you need to be competent on how you make plans for your daily tasks. If unsure about things in any situation you'll find the Internet is nearby and usually there are always people around willing to help you out.

Teaching others or yourself to learn new machines could be a massive time saver boost for production work you may need. For instance an electric clothing material cutter only takes seconds to use compared to hand cutting material with scissors.

Even simple devices can save you time so always try and think of ways you can automate or use technology to your favour. Sometimes just bringing in say an extra table can give you more space to work on more freely and do jobs faster for instance.

Stress Management

Managing stress at home or in the workplace is very important as you need to have outlets and breaks no matter how much time you think you're saving. People need their breaks, days off and holidays. You have to make time to unwind and have fun. Getting obsessed with your job or home tasks will eventually affect your health.

So you need to make time for relaxation and personal alone time. We all need a break and time management is part of that. Doing things smarter using others around you, using machines and technology will give you that time to relax and relieve the stress you may have built up during any period.

If you get tired at nights don't always push your limits just to watch a TV show for instance. Take the sleep when you need it the most. I quiet often just put my feet up in the chair and close my eyes for some super relaxation breaks which may only be for 15 or 20 minutes. Even short breaks like that will help you to get through the tired and stressful times. Pushing yourself beyond your limit is like trying to run your car without oil. Eventually you'll just burn out.

You can't let the pressures and things get to you and managing your anger is part of that. Again you need to know when to step back and take a deep breath and take things in their stride. If you can accept things will not always go to plan you'll find you'll be able to deal with most situations quiet well. Machines may break down for instance and running around cursing, waving your arms about or taking it out on others isn't any solution. You just have to accept it as it is and do what you can to get things operating again to how you need them to be.

Time management is also about problem solving. If you've learnt anything from this book so far you'd notice it's all about problem solving. Finding solutions to anything that's thrown in your way and looking for options to change how things are organized. Everything is about using organizational skills. Everything is about learning how to use those skills to adapt other actions to change things to how you need them to be. Changing your home and work practices so you can move forward. Bad things will always happen and at the most inconvenient times.

Knowing how to solve those issues is what's important. By all means throw a minor tantrum or say some choice swear words to yourself but then pick yourself right up and solve the problem without wasting any more time on it. Get over it as crap happens to all of us and you're no exception.

Always keep in mind some solutions that can help you along can be hired very quickly sometimes. Get a repair person in, hire a temporary machine or sometimes it just may be cheaper to replace the issue. I'm sure if you stay calm you'll find the solution much faster than if you lose your head and fly off the handle.

Stay Focused

Always keep good records if you're in business so then that way you can keep track not only of your own performance but also that of your employees. Even in the home situation keep track of yourself so that you don't slip back into your old ways of doing things like wasting and losing too much time. Like I've said before it can be an addiction habit once you start doing things the wrong way and you regress.

In business always use production charts and keep records of actual production and work on ways to improve that to the best possible outcome. Sometime that may mean updating to a better machine for instance and even swapping staff around to someone that may be more suited to that style of work. You have to accept that every person is different and people have different attitudes in how they work. Some will always perform better than others and some may perform better than you. People aren't machines and their personal output will always vary. Try and pick the best people out of who you have.

Naturally don't fight the unachievable. People aren't machines and we can only do what we can do. Make sure you always prioritize your work and home tasks in the best possible order. A simple example is if you need to wash clothes and it needs all day to dry then there's no point washing late in the day. Simple common sense in the work place is the same. Naturally if orders are waiting for specific items then you try and always get those orders done first. Priority is very important.

Develop and organize time saving habits like keeping things in their right place so you don't have to waste time searching for basic things. Everything in the right place makes a good home and business environment. Forgetting where you place your reading glasses for instance is a favorite for many people no doubt. Keep your keys in the same place. Place tools back where they belong.

Having a to-do list ready in the morning will help you keep focused on all your tasks be that in the home, school or at work. Straying off the beaten path is so easy and usually means you can expect to get very little done for that day. You need to motivate yourself to be specific about your daily tasks. Ask yourself questions in your mind. Keep a written record of your daily achievements if this helps you. In business you should make that a requirement. Keeping good records is a time saver not a waste of time. Be dedicated and responsible every day for all your tasks. There's no one to blame but yourself and there's nothing wrong with stuffing up sometimes. People aren't machines and they can't compete against that.

Don't drink heavily or take drugs and expect the next day to be good for you or anyone else as that will most likely impair any tasks you must do. Doing excess is never a good way to wind down thinking that's your way to relaxation. There's always a price to pay for that. Snacking too much during the day can also be a distraction. Try and keep your eating to your break times.

There's nothing wrong with sharing your thoughts with others in the workplace or telling some jokes for fun as long as it's not at the expense of others. You need little breaks like that during the day so you don't go round the twist. And if you do feel sick or have health issues its okay to tell others. That relieves some that stress on your mind. A problem told is a problem shared. Everyone has issues at different times.

I know many books and people will tell you to follow a strict timetable but I'm of the mind yes by all means follow a schedule but don't let it take over your whole life. You can only perform or work to your own personal capabilities and if you do your best that's all anyone can expect of you. Naturally if you try and put it over others expect to get whatever is due to you. Always be honest and stay true to your work area be it at home or in a business.

A time table to me is nothing more than a rough guide for those that have trouble planning their time management. You need the ability to plan ahead of your needs. In fact you need to be able to predict a future need for your day and weeks task needs. So like a mind reader your predicting what will save you time by organizing your task needs be that at home or in the work place.

In the workplace if you have say have a concreting job to do you need to make sure you order a concrete truck to coincide with the time you'll be ready to pour the concrete. You'll need to check the weather, make sure that if it did rain you have a contingency plan in place like with covers for the project for instance. Make sure the work site is ready to pour concrete not that you keep the truck waiting.

Make sure you have all the tools and people needed on site. Have all the materials for the job and you need to think it all out beforehand to save yourself time and hold ups. Then make sure that if there's some concrete left over have somewhere it may be of use ready. Even many builders fall for that one. There may be concrete left over and it would be a waste just to dump it. Have a hose nearby for cleaning things down etc. Have people there onsite to finish off the concrete when it's ready.

It's about pre-empting what needs to be done and factoring in other things that may come to pass as well. Organizing and being prepared will save you lots of running around and time. If you leave your planning to chance and doing your planning on the spot you'll probably find you'll always forget the fine details and you'll be left on the spot running around wasting heaps of time. We've all been through that trying to do last minute changes.

This is why I like to just spend basically seconds in bed in the early morning planning my day in advance so I don't have to worry about forgetting last minute things and losing more time. As you get used to working this way you'll probably find yourself feeling sort of invincible because you'll have everything placed as it should be for many jobs.

In employment it will save you lots of time and make you more money due to those lost periods of wasted time. You'll tighten up the whole process of pre-thinking and for the needs of others around you including yourself. Even if something goes wrong you can factor in alternatives to do other things so you don't lose much time.

So your planning doesn't need to mean you have to have a strict work timetable as a timetable to me is just a rough guide. By all means try and set yourself time guides but be flexible enough to work around them if things don't happen on time. Trucks may get held up for instance, have a flat tyre or breakdown. So a smarter time manager will have alternative things ready to do in advance no matter what happens. Have other jobs to do while waiting.

Always have alternative plans where possible just in case. Even in the home situation if something turns up out of the blue so be prepared to change your plans for that day or that time and factor in other things to do. Unexpected things can happen at any time and how you manage them will mean the difference between getting behind in those things or just getting on with an alternative option.

There are nearly always alternative things to do in our lives and workplace. If you don't have much time left do some of those less important jobs you've been putting off for instance.

To me time management isn't just about watching a clock. It's about preparation of your days activities. So many stay at home people and those in the workplace can't organize their activities. And this is where the time just gets sucked away from you. In the workplace you also need to make sure your employees are motivated to work. If you continually stuff them around by say not having things ready for them to do you'll find that those people will get used to that and just naturally take their time. It's hard to restore confidence in workers that don't respect you.

But if you always make sure that have a constant flow of work to do they won't have a reason to lag behind and do nothing. It's a lot to do with your attitude so you need to set the example of always having work to do and be busy. Always organizing and setting jobs in place for others to do in advance. This is your job and that of others you delegate too.

I've always had an ability to walk into most work places and find easier and different ways to do things to get better results like an intuition. Time management is simply that. Finding ways to better the time it takes to do specific tasks. That may mean changing or even designing new technology like say redesigning a machine or even a whole new manufacturing process.

I've done this and many other people have done the same. For example on a farm for instance redesigning new machinery applicable to specific tasks can save you thousands in labour hours.

Picking potatoes by hand or digging and collecting them by machine for example. That's a massive time and labour saving process.

And even in an office there are many ways you can save time and labour when you start thinking about different ways of doing things. Sometimes it may mean some new computer software or training people differently. There can be many different options where time management comes into play. The advent of so much technology now can have many time saving devices at hand.

Remember if you have to pay for employee hours it's in your interest to find better ways to do the same job. New developments can come into play at any time so you need to keep on top of this. Technology is your best friend at home and at work. It's quicker for some people with limited time to say use a clothes dryer than manually hang the washing out and collect it again. Everyone can make choices to see what suits their personal position the best. Editing your lifestyle preferences is about time management.

If you don't have time to do specific things look for a time saving option and that may mean delegating jobs out to others, improving technology or basically just planning your day better. We all must make choices everyday of our lives and how you plan those choices can make a huge difference.

Take Time Out To Be A Human

We all make mistakes, get behind on jobs, need mental time outs and have to deal with all manner of crisis. Negative events can drain your personality and turn you into a nervous wreck if you let it. Always step back and relook at any situation. Is it really a life or death situation? Or will it just mean it's a hold up in time?

So it's going to be late or take longer. Is that really worth stressing about? As a time manager you should now be able to deal with any situation. It may be a pain and even hold a lot of people up so it's better to keep a cool head and look for alternatives. Find other jobs for people to do. Find something else for you to do. Design concepts for that scenario in your head before these things happen.

If say it's in a sawmill and your main machine has broken down and it will take weeks to get parts to fix what would you do? Sit there stressing about it or look for a way to keep your workforce working? There are always work-around solutions even if that means subletting some jobs out to keep production going. It may cost you more but at least you may not lose your customer base. You may be able to hire a portable onsite machine to keep work going until repairs and parts can be done.

The world around you doesn't have to stop when something goes wrong. Ideally as a time management operator you should look into that scenario well before things like that happen. Surely you must know if your whole workforce is dependent on say one main machine you need to have arrangements in place so if that machine breaks down that you can implement at short notice. That's important time management planning. If you are in charge this is your job to know and to do that.

In business and in the home there may be many alternatives like rental machines, buying a secondhand back up item, repair, insurance or whatever. Industrial machinery auctions are often an alternative worth thinking about before something bad happens in your workplace.

Sometimes it may be an affordable back up plan you need to consider rather than leaving things to chance. You're the time manager so just image how much it will cost you if something major happens in your workplace and you don't have a quick alternative ready to take over. Can you really afford that loss?
In say an office a printer may pack it in and a couple of hundred will fix that quick by just going out to buy another. Not every issue has to be so major so having the ability to adapt to problems is a

very good skill to have and learn. You must become your own problem solver in the home or at work.

Make sure you take the time to always have breaks during the day. We all need rest downtime. You're no good to anyone including yourself if you're wound up tight like a spring in a clock. That spring will only break over time if you don't unwind. Stress is a major downfall for many of us if we don't take enough time out. People aren't machines.

Changing Habits, Patterns And Your Thinking

We as humans can actually change the way we do things but sometimes it takes a push in the right direction or even just a little teaching of different concepts to show you how to make that change. That's what this book is about. Learning to adapt and create your own change of direction in life. Most of us can learn to rearrange our lives if we want too. Some of us torture ourselves into stressful situations because we choose not to change.

Placing burdens and barriers in our own way for some is a way of life but that doesn't mean we can't change that. In most cases people never stop learning throughout their life. You may not realize it but you're being taught to do new things every day. If there's roadworks along a road and a detour sign is placed there you're shown or being taught to go another way for instance. It may not seem like you're being taught something new but it changed your mind from a habit you may have been used too. Time management is no different. It's a detour in your life adjusting the way you do things to take you on a different journey. It's a different way to what you're used to.

Tic Tic Tic and time passes as we get older and we can't change that direction no matter how hard we try. Our clocks are counting down for all of us. But what we can do is maximize the use of some of that time to our advantage. As you get older you come to realize we aren't immortal and time seems to pass much faster as age creeps upon you. For children time may seem to pass much slower. Now in my 60's years seem to pass very quickly for me and even though I've maximized the way I do things time still passes very quickly for me. Everyone is different and for you it may not seem that way.

Either way I like to make the best use of my time so I can try and fit more into my days. There are those that just want life to go away and I can understand that if their personal lives may not be as fulfilling as that of others. Those in age care homes may just want it over for instance. Being very old or sick for some is torture. So we all have to deal with our own version of time. Many people don't care if their personal tasks stretch out over a whole day because it fills out their day for them. And for some they just can't seem to fit enough into each day.

And for them time management is crucial because it can turn them into a stressful mess if they need to keep worrying about how to get their tasks done. Time management is about relieving those pressures by planning better ways to maximize your time. Taking that pressure away can be a huge burden lifted out of some people's lives. By showing how to plan your days differently I hope I can teach you to teach yourself how to do that. Reorganizing, delegate jobs to others, plan in advance can all take these pressures out of your daily life. If you can organize someone to do your lawn mowing, laundry, ironing, housework, take your kids to schools, or whatever these are all time saving measures.

Some you may have to pay for and some you may be able to barter with others. It doesn't matter if the end result gives you more time and peace of mind to live a more productive life free from some of the pressures around you. It may not be the golden cure for all your issues but no matter what you personally need to feel less stress in your life.

Prioritize Your Tasks

No matter what we all like to choose what we like to do best first and that's human nature. I suppose if everyone thought that way many of us would be on holidays most of the time. But life places burdens upon us like deadlines and finish dates so we already know these jobs must take priority over others right?

But breaking that barrier to allocate enough time to complete those tasks for many people is a huge burden. They may have sports training, a date or other fun things to do and they usually end up putting those things first leaving those deadlines to mount up till it's too late to grab that lost time back. I'm sure many of us have been guilty of doing the wrong things at the wrong times.

In the case of say studying for exams or delivering specific results it could affect your future or that of other people so we all know that wouldn't be fair on anyone. If you say have an assignment to write its best to write it in sections rather than try and push it all out at once. And if you're like me you'll most likely find the little time in between can actually work to your advantage and you'll most likely think of better aspects to add to that assignment making it a better overall achievement on your part. Break things down into achievable goals when you can.

Doing everything in one go isn't always the best approach to completion. You may forget important parts, it may look hurried and overall it may show you didn't give it your best.   That could mean lower marks in school or even the loss of your job. For instance I'm writing this book in sections that suit my mood. It gives me time to reflect on what I'm writing. There's no rush or time frame for me personally so why should I push this project before others?

You need to work in the right conditions to suit your application. You can't always force yourself to get good results. You need to work more naturally so what you produce can be seen to be well thought out and researched as it needs to be done. A hurried project will usually produce mistakes and factors you never counted on. You need to take a step back and keep your goals in perspective to the needs of each project you undertake. Everything you undertake may have some level of consequences that may affect you or others.

Plan your projects well in advance and allow yourself the right amount of proper allocated time or times as required. If we could all redo parts of our lives many of us would say "if only I prepared myself better for that specific project I wouldn't being living like this today". Well we can't turn back the hands of time but we can plan better for the future with better time management. And for some you can perhaps still change your future into something better.

Students

By planning the best time for you to undertake specific tasks could mean the difference between a different future in your life so you need to recognize the importance of time management for many things you undertake in your life.

Students for instance need to apply time management for writing their projects, exams and for other important tasks they may need to perform and manage. If you need to write down a timetable to help you manage your assignments do that and remember that if you stray from doing your most important tasks first they could have life changing consequences.

If you find your workload is high it may pay to break it down into sections so that way you can leave some time in between to have short breaks, a drink or a snack to boost you up again. Even a 5 minute power nap can help you keep interested and motivated to complete each task.

It may seem like the pressure is on but breaking it down into workable units may just help you cope. Allocate the time you need and not the time you want to waste for specific tasks. By all means be flexible as you always want to give your best for all the things you undertake. Sometimes if you have the time it may pay to do more the next day giving you a fresh perspective of your assignment and perhaps some time in between to do some extra research you think may be needed.

Thinking about some things in your off period can sometimes help a lot. Choose your study space wisely so you're free to work without distractions, mobile phones and people that can interrupt your lines of thought. It's so easy to get distracted and then to try and get back into that flow zone may be near impossible.

The best thing about modern technology is that you can keep copies of your work on computers for review. It always pays to review your assignments because if you're like me you can always think of something else you'd like to add just to make it just that little bit better. Let's not even talk about typos and grammar mistakes.

If you have a close friend that can proof read for you that would be great. No one is perfect and there's nothing wrong with asking for a little help when needed. Naturally do your hardest assignments first because that's when you'll be the most alert. Sometimes you'll need to sacrifice recreation times to complete more important tasks that should have priority. That's life I'm afraid.

When you do get some free time make sure you use it wisely. Get the break you need but that doesn't mean you still can't think about your study and school work options while you're say going for a walk. Sometimes you can solve issues you're having by having breaks and changing your way of thinking.

Don't forget to keep track of your specific subjects and lecture material. You don't want to end up forgetting that information because you weren't prioritizing the right tasks at the right time. It's all too easy to pick your favorite subjects rather than what should be done first. Taking the easy way out could cost you big time if you forget some of the most important work. Always keep lecture notes as that can save you time remembering and help you jog your memory of the most important things. By doing that it may just help you do some other subjects at different times.

Researching what you can from varied resources can give you different perspectives on specialized subjects. The list of available resources can be massive these days. Time management can be crucial if you have several projects due at similar times.

Plan – Prioritize – Organize. Will be your guide throughout major studies because if you can't implement the time management skills I've outlined you'll most likely find yourself floundering through some subjects. If you don't use your time wisely you'll most likely regret it later.

Effective Planning

If your time management is working well for you you'll most likely find you have time to spare and that could end up being 50% more than you originally thought. This is where you need to make sure you're not over confident. Things go wrong and sometimes you may need a lot more time than you think to finish some tasks. Interruptions have a way of growing out of control.

By all means make good use of your saved time but don't sacrifice everything on some poor decisions and regret it later. You may have a great timetable but sometimes what you need to do is take on tomorrow's tasks earlier. Especially if you know it's something that may give you some problems. Or say if it's something you don't like doing. Over estimating a time gain on one day doesn't always mean the same will happen the next day.

You'll have to learn what to balance out or what to take a chance on. Rarely do things always work out 100% perfect which means you may need some extra time spent in other areas on other days. Again you have to become the mind reader and estimate what's more important at the time. If you know you have really difficult tasks coming up it may be better to play it on the safe side and use at least some of that spare time making a start on the next task.

Learn to say no to some things if you know you have more important things to do first. You'll soon learn to balance recreational activities in your spare time to your advantage after some practice as you devise your own work timetables and programs.

Everything comes down to what's most important to you. Prioritize things the best way you can. Reorganize recreation where possible as there are lots of days and times in the week you can do that. People will understand as others have to do the same. People can't always drop whatever they're doing to take time off from their tasks.

Sometimes jobs, education and things at home must take priority over everything else for you. You can't always worry what someone else may think as we all have to live our own lives.

Everyone is different and what other people get away with may not work for you so be extra careful. Losing your future to just do silly things may not be a good investment for you to undertake.

Time Management For Young Children

It may sound over the top but teaching very basic time management to young kids is a great place to ground them for the future. Once kids learn to start telling the time is around the best time to teach them. Simply start with bed, washing, eating, reading, dressing, school and play times etc.

Tell them the time on the clock and associate the task to do those things at similar times every day. You'll be amazed at how fast kids adapt to timetable management learning. It teaches kids routines to live by. It's all time management brought down to a basic level that kids can relate too. All manner of tasks can be built into those routines. If you have disabled children it can help them enormously sometimes as many kids actually like routines as it gives them something to look forward to at different times.

As an adult it pays to check out how your time management programs are working for you. Are you allowing enough time for breaks for instance not that you just keep plugging away pushing yourself to your limit? It's important to be flexible and plan to change your plan as required. Not everything you set out has to be set in stone.

You have a whole week to plan for specific tasks and if done well you should always have time left over. Use that spare time wisely. Decide what's most important to you personally. Is your time management making a difference in your life? If it is working for you obviously it will make a huge breakthrough in your life because this will take some of the everyday stress burden away from you.

Looking Back At Your Time Savings

Finding ways to get more done and to save time may have a different meaning to many of us.

At home it may help you find time to go out and enjoy some of your favourite pastimes.

As a student it may help organize and regulate a program so you can submit better quality assignments on time and retain information better.

In the workplace it may help you produce more output thereby reducing your cost per item. Time savings then becomes a crucial profit driven criteria for manufacturing and production.

In all cases it allows you to allocate time in areas of your specific goals and interests. It makes you the master of your own fate and it can reduce stressful situations by better planning for things that may or may not happen.

You'll teach yourself to delegate jobs to others if or when needed. You'll learn how to train yourself and others to make time savings measures.

You'll learn to set aside time for recreation and family which is an important factor in most of our lives. Setting these goals in place isn't always about making money. It can be about opening up more avenues of quality in your life.

Reducing stress also plays an important part of time management. Many times just taking those 30 seconds of thought to decide how you'll do some specific tasks can change your whole life.

Thinking and planning ahead of your daily tasks can save you so much time because you'll be more organized and you can imagine how you'll set your day out to fit specific tasks in place.

I hope these methods can get you motivated into changing the way you do your everyday tasks.

Good luck with your time management.